ALISON WILDING
IMMERSION/EXPOSURE

TATE GALLERY LIVERPOOL / HENRY MOORE SCULPTURE TRUST STUDIO

ACKNOWLEDGEMENTS

The artist would like to thank all those who have assisted with *Immersion* and *Exposure*.

Special thanks to: Susan Crowe, Stephen Park, Steve Turner at Heights Design (Halifax), Mentmore Sculpture Services (London), Ian Mitchell at G Robinson Fabrications Ltd (Halifax), Theoplastic Ltd (Barking), John Rowe

ISBN 1-85437-078-2

Published by order of the Trustees 1991 for the exhibition *Alison Wilding Immersion: Sculpture from Ten Years* 22 May – 4 August 1991 Selected by Lewis Biggs and Alison Wilding

This exhibition coincides with an installation of new works entitled *Exposure* which will be on view from 6 June – 11 August 1991 at the Henry Moore Sculpture Trust Studio, Dean Clough, Halifax

Edited by Penelope Curtis Prepared by Tate Gallery Liverpool, Albert Dock, Liverpool L3 4BB Designed by Jeremy Greenwood, Woodbridge Colour origination by Primary Four Ltd. Moreton, Wirral Printed in Great Britain by Printfine Limited, Liverpool

ILLUSTRATION CREDITS

Susan Ormerod, London, England pp11 lower, 12, 12, 13, 13, 14 upper, 15 lower, 16 lower, 17 centre, 35, 37, 41, 43, 45, 51, 53, 55, 57 FRAC des Pays de la Loire, France pp 15, 47 Art Gallery of New South Wales, Australia p14 Alex Hartley p59 Jerry Hardman-Jones, Leeds, pp66-72, back cover

Front cover
Detail, *Stormy Weather* 1987

Back cover
Detail, *Stain* 1991

CONTENTS

Preface   5

IMMERSION

Sayings   8
Greg Hilty

List of works   18

Plates   20

EXPOSURE

Alison Wilding interviewed by Greg Hilty   62
7 June 1991

List of works   65

Plates   66

BIOGRAPHY & BIBLIOGRAPHY   74

4

PREFACE

Alison Wilding participated in the opening exhibition at Tate Gallery Liverpool, *Starlit Waters*, which showed some of the sculpture from Britain which has excited international interest over the last two decades. Her work began to attract attention a decade ago, and has continued to elicit admiration, especially from other artists, ever since. In the early 1980s her sculptures were seen in the Biennales in Paris and Sao Paolo, and in solo exhibitions in New York and Venice.

While she has continued to exhibit widely in other countries her only exhibition in a public gallery in this country has been at the Serpentine Gallery in London in 1985. Since then, her work has continued to grow in ambition, confidence and precision, and we invited her to make this exhibition at Tate Gallery Liverpool in the belief that her work deserves wider appreciation in this country.

In the 1970s, Alison Wilding's work took the form of environmental installation. As she began to make objects for exhibition, the experience and aims of her earlier work remained constant. She incorporates a measured sense of time into her sculpture. In contrast to that of many artists who search for immediacy of image and expression, her work reveals itself to us slowly, and is highly sensitive to its surroundings. This exhibition should bring a deeper knowledge of her work and a greater enjoyment of it to a large and new audience.

We hope that a number of visitors to the exhibition in Liverpool will also see the display of Alison Wilding's new large-scale sculptures at the Henry Moore Sculpture Trust Studio in Dean Clough in Halifax, which runs concurrently. We are grateful to Robert Hopper, Director of the Henry Moore Sculpture Trust, for his suggestion that we should collaborate on the production of this publication, the costs of which have been supported by the Henry Moore Foundation. We owe thanks to Greg Hilty for his imaginative text which complements the reproductions, and to Karsten Schubert and Richard Salmon for their help with information on the artist.

We have gathered together sculptures from private collections in Europe and the United States as well as in England, and we acknowledge with gratitude the trust and generosity accorded us by the lenders to the exhibition. Above all we thank Alison Wilding for accepting the invitation to exhibit and for engaging with the gallery and its public so wholeheartedly.

Nicholas Serota
Director, Tate Gallery

Lewis Biggs
Curator, Tate Gallery Liverpool

IMMERSION

TATE GALLERY LIVERPOOL

SAYINGS

Greg Hilty

'Thy lips are like a thread of scarlet, and thy speech is comely: thy temples are like a piece of pomegranate within thy locks./ Thy neck is like the tower of David builded for an armoury, whereon there hang a thousand buckles, all shields of mighty men'.[1]

These two verses from 'The Song of Solomon' are typical of its most frequent use of metaphor: the listing of multiple attributes, often wildly exaggerated, as signs of a boundless fascination or love expressed through repeated transference.

There is a second kind that does not seek to build up such a complex, saturated image, but instead equates two separate images: 'We have a little sister, and she hath no breasts: what shall we do for our sister in the day when she shall be spoken for?/ If she be a wall, we will build upon her a palace of silver: and if she be a door, we will inclose her with boards of cedar'.[2]

This dynamic of equivalence rather than comparison, instead of heightening our understanding of what the words describe, explodes the descriptive words themselves. To say 'our little sister' is 'a wall' does not allow our mind's eye to focus on a grammatical pairing or succession of images: it oscillates instead between the two images in linguistic, visual and emotional agitation. This can create a site for fusion, for new thoughts to emerge and to take form.

1. 'The Song of Solomon' 4:3 & 4, Authorized Version of the Bible

2. *ibid,* 8:8 & 9

The substitution in Alison Wilding's 'Scree' of sand and pigment for an accumulation of stones or debris on the slope of a hill is not an image but an equivalent. It is, and is also like, a slice of the world contained. But its confinement is dynamic, its substance is about to pour out. This is the eternal tension of a work of art, to hold within itself so much potential, whether of brute material or of loaded meanings. We could talk of an 'imploded field of sculpture', or of embodiment. The object has a latent energy which can burst forth on looking, in perception, and in the release of memories or associations.

This small work is placed well above eye level on the wall, establishing a formal sense of proportion within the gallery but also using height as a material component of the piece, like brass or paint.

An 'Untitled' sculpture of 1981 is made of black cast silk and brass painted black, mirror images of darkness, one warm, one cold, like a slice of night-time shadow in a darkened corner of the building that has cast it. The whole tapers gently towards the top, like a tower or a chimney. These images are only projections, and others would be possible. We have to engage actively with its own language, to allow this small black object on the wall to speak for itself.

Wilding's sculptures demand to be viewed metaphorically. They are normally made of familiar materials, often disguised or oddly juxtaposed, and we naturally wonder why. This urge to understand is seldom satisfied, however. These works cannot be read, although interpretations can be teased out or invented. It seems that just as often as they evoke physical or emotional states (or at the same time), their real subject is the difficulty of bearing or transferring meaning itself.

'In the lee of the island I hear your voice, deep inside the calm'.[3] With a few small words from a popular song our senses are flooded: space, place, voice, depth and atmosphere are conflated in a single lilting line, which is then repeated for good measure.

3. 'The Mariner's Song' by The Cowboy Junkies

'Well' establishes its own interior space, a territory in a curve of steel. From within this protective embrace protrudes an embryonic shape, striving for definition. Its hollowed-out underside contributes to the physical description of what the shape might be, but also suggests a private space that need not be described.

There is an intriguing level of artifice in Alison Wilding's works. They often seem purer and more direct than they really are. Wood is in fact always carved and often painted, metal cut and bent and burnished.

When we say two things are like chalk and cheese, we really mean that they are as unlike each other as chalk and cheese are. This is a negative metaphor, a simile of dissimilarity.

The underside of 'Beneath the Skin' is significant: it is like seeing inside a rock. The outer surface of what is in fact a rounded lump of oak bears evidence of several holes, efforts to penetrate, to understand its brute obtuseness. These explorations are carried almost but not quite through to the hollow, and are filled with healing beeswax, as if she has had second thoughts and tried to make amends.

The wooden part of 'Plunder' is black walnut, its shape that of a bow-tie or propeller, its surface gently modulated. Stuffed within is a piece of Irish linen, like a secondary vision, a denser understanding that circulates around and fills the sculpted wood, articulating its unseen centre. This of course involves a kind of invasion, perhaps referred to by the title. The linen takes on a form determined partly by the walnut and partly by the bulges and creases that are the consequences of its own material properties.

The bowl of 'Hemlock' forms a space for contrasts, a mortar holding lead and beeswax. This rests in turn precariously on a kind of ledge, in a perfect poise that is part of an equation of becoming. There is tension between word and object, between contrasting materials, between balancing objects. They could fall apart, but they don't.

All of these works form a concerted revolt against stasis, against standing still and its mental equivalent, one-track thinking. Their poise is delicate, their meanings hard won. They are small but robust. Seldom complicated, they are nevertheless difficult in a way that only the right and the obvious can be.

The rightness embodied in each work is not a final, conclusive prescription, but a material adage whose truth we never tire of.

Tektite is described as 'a glassy body of probably meteoric origin and of rounded but indefinite shape... found especially in Czechoslovakia, Indonesia and

Australia.' A piece of it forms the core of 'Fruit', around which wind interlocking thin brass rods, more like an energy field than an organic outgrowing. This suggests a kind of transparency, something hidden and something to get through.

The much larger floor piece called 'Blue Skies' also has a stone core at its centre, a rounded piece of Cornish granite. It, too, is protected: invisible from the sides, seen but inaccessible from both ends, hemmed in by two symmetric, interlocking metal structures in a symbolic closed circuit.

'Into the Brass' operates like a cloak and cupboard magic act. Its deception is casual but complete. The cloth, pierced to heighten the mystery of what's beneath it (the brass shines through like an inner source of light), performs a contrary function to that of the lighter coloured cloth of 'Plunder': an active agent of mystery and concealment, rather than of comprehension. Something hard possessing volume and a distinctive shape is transformed into a darkly shimmering, fluid, indefinite substance.

The contrasting movements of thrusting outwards and plunging in are central to many of Wilding's works, notably the brass piece 'Immersion'. More recently, she has turned her attention to moving through material in other ways, to the subtler penetration and quieter contrasts of transparency and opacity. The sense remains one of uncovering, or of coming into being.

'Seal' offers three examples of form appearing to emerge. First: a block of sandstone, rough-hewn and of irregular dimensions. Second, by contrast: a perfectly formed and hard-edged but semi-transparent tower of white polypropylene. And finally: the conjunction of the two, the border where their matter commingles, the blurred half-presence of the sandstone seen through plastic.

There is an earlier echo of this relation in 'Receiver', where oak nudges up against and into a galvanized steel tower. Poise and interdependence are equated once again.

'Displace' is composed of two distinct elements joined together: a black steel tower (like one half of the early black 'Untitled' piece considerably magnified), and a polypropylene accretion sprouting out of it. This extension takes the form of three repeated segments of the same shape but of diminishing size, like ever-fainter memories or projections from the tower. It is a crystalline expansion out into new territory, a polymerization of thought.

'Stormy Weather' could be read as an almost theatrically descriptive piece. With its steel grey skies, its lightning zigzag join, and the chaos of a storm pictured in its cast bronze floor, it makes a little atmospheric *mise-en-scène*. Like gods we can stick our heads into this self-contained catastrophe and observe the drama, the dumb dialogue between two opposing fronts, monoliths of different character but the same nature, and the chaos trapped between them.

But which way round does the metaphor work? Perhaps the atmospheric comparison is meant to tell us something instead about sculpture or art, about balance again, and the tension between two objects, about the quiet harmony of this relation and on the other hand the electric storm of associations and ideas that can be generated by it.

The storm itself, its cast bronze image, in turn suggests alternative images: water when the tide has broken, rain on a puddle, molten lava, tar on a road in summer, melted ice-cream, bubbling soup, spilled paint, burnt plastic.

In the later work 'Fuse' the same two shapes seem reconciled, holding each other in perfect mutual support with an unseen intimate space between them.

This private space is most completely expressed in the almost figurative sculptures 'Vestal', 'Her Furnace', and 'Nest'. It is a space of heat and of creation.

The act of understanding (and probably also that of making) the work 'Fuse' involves something like a rocking motion between questions and answers, between almost simultaneous pain and pleasure. Although it would be possible to talk about it like other works - in terms of material, metaphor, image, containment, poise, and so on - the reasons for its success seem literally indescribable. Every decision that has gone into its making is an avoidance of superfluity. Yet it is not simply minimal: its form remains alive with these decisions, held in such tenuous balance that to describe would be to over-burden them.

This is not to deny the need to search for a language that lends definition to works that themselves give body to some of our deepest, if simplest, emotions. A language that neither explains nor fails to explain, but somehow surrounds the work in attempting to understand it. That follows its contours and feels its rough and smooth surfaces, weighing its material and stalking its territory. And finally respecting the private space which neither touch, nor sight, nor words can fully comprehend.

1 *Untitled* 1981
   Copper, silk and wood
   508 x 102 x 102mm
   Private Collection

2 *Green Beak* 1983
   Slate and patinated copper
   580 x 160 x 140mm
   Arts Council Collection, South Bank Centre, London

3 *Scree* 1984
   Coloured copper, brass, sand and pigment
   205 x 230 x 270mm
   Collection Bianca Attolico, Rome

4 *Well* 1985
   Leaded steel, limewood and paint
   400 x 292 x 140mm
   Collection Cosmo Rodewald

5 *Vestal* 1985
   Brass
   1065 x 390 x 185mm
   Collection the Artist

6 *Hearth* 1986
   Brass, copper, leaded steel and pigment
   2085 x 407 x 965mm
   Private Collection

7 *Beneath the Skin* 1986
   Wood and wax
   285 x 673 x 127mm
   Collection Martin Kunz, New York/Basel

8 *Her Furnace* 1986-7
   Copper and brass
   865 x 395 x 355mm
   Private Collection

9 *Hemlock III* 1986
   Limewood, hemlock, lead, beeswax and pigment
   185 x 145 x 90mm
   Collection Richard Salmon, London
   (Courtesy Karsten Schubert Ltd., London)

10 *Nest* 1986
Copper and Issore marble
600 x 325 x 320mm
Private Collection, Sussex

11 *Blue Skies* 1987
500 x 2840 x 1320mm
Galvanised steel, Cornish granite and nickel silver
Private Collection loan to Southampton City Art
Gallery

12 *Into the Brass* 1987
Brass and wool/cotton cloth
910 x 2050 x 1230mm
Karsten Schubert Ltd., London

13 *Immersion* 1988
Brass
997 x 483 x 559mm
The Edward R Broida Trust

14 *Receiver* 1988
Oak, galvanised steel, pigment and beeswax
1945 x 1405 x 1000mm
Karsten Schubert Ltd., London

15 *Stormy Weather* 1987
Galvanised steel, oil paint and bronze
2248 x 1156 x 1702mm
Weltkunst Foundation, Zurich

16 *Possession* 1989
Oak, utile wax and oil paint
311 x 686 x 235mm
Private Collection, Tennessee

17 *Displace* 1990
Polypropylene, steel and rubber
2184 x 1930 x 978mm
Karsten Schubert Ltd., London

18 *Fuse* 1990
Polypropylene and leaded steel
1778 x 1219 x 1753mm
Karsten Schubert Ltd., London

19 *Fruit* 1990
Brass and tektite
101 x 101 x 89mm
Private Collection, London

20 *Tidal* 1990-91
Steel, brass and rubber
1840 x 2260 x 790mm
Courtesy the Artist and Karsten Schubert Ltd.,
London

1. *Untitled* 1981

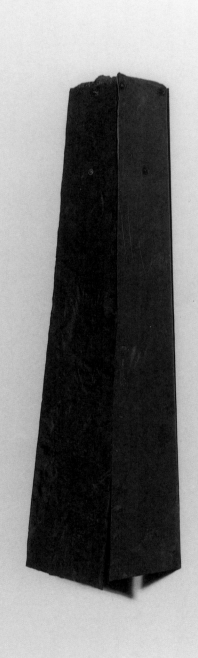

2. *Green Beak* 1983

3. *Scree* 1984

4. *Well* 1985

5. *Vestal* 1985

6. *Hearth* 1986

7. *Beneath the Skin* 1986

8. *Her Furnace* 1986-7

9. *Hemlock III* 1986

10. *Nest* 1986

11. *Blue Skies* 1987

12. *Into the Brass* 1987

13. *Immersion* 1988

14. *Receiver* 1988

15. *Stormy Weather* 1987

16. *Possession* 1989

17. *Displace* 1990

18. *Fuse* 1990

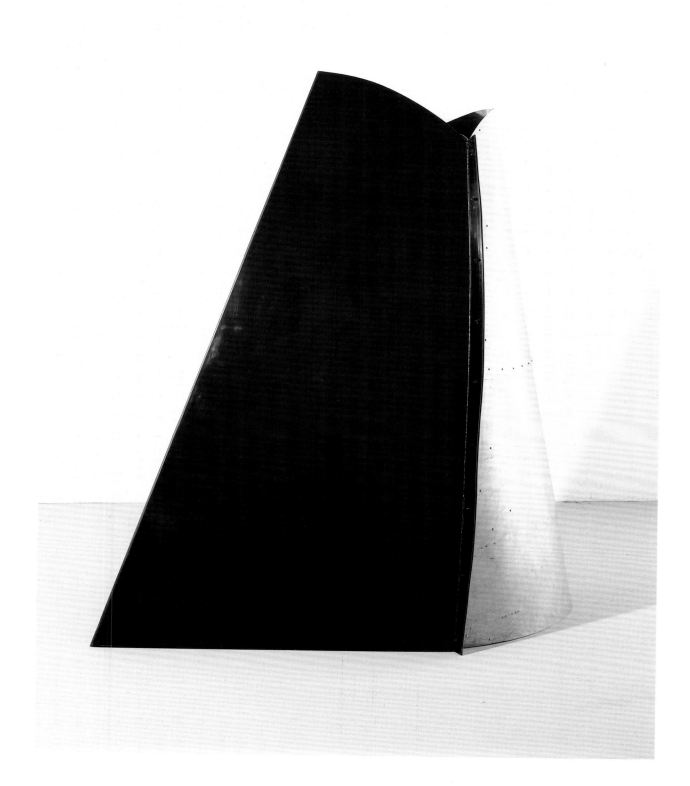

19. *Fruit* 1990

20. *Tidal* 1990-91

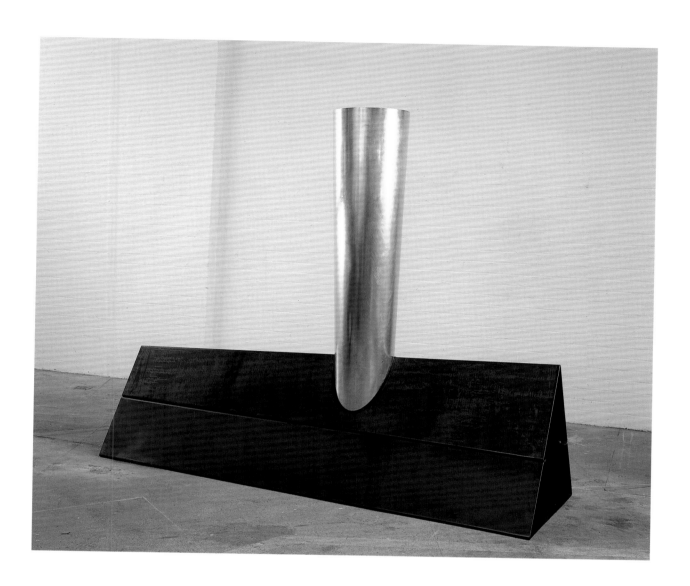

EXPOSURE

HENRY MOORE SCULPTURE TRUST STUDIO

ALISON WILDING INTERVIEWED BY GREG HILTY

7 June 1991

GH: Had you ever thought of making work on a very large scale before being invited to by the Henry Moore Sculpture Trust? Have you ever made an installation?

AW: A lot of the work I made in the early 70s, soon after I left the Royal College, would probably now be regarded as installation. It was quite unsuccessful. The artists who I shared a studio block with didn't like it. I didn't try to explain anything, I simply presented it and if it worked for myself, that was fine.

GH: Did it have its antecedents in sculpture or installation, or were the two indistinguishable at that time?

AW: I don't think that was part of the argument. Sculpture was in what you would call a very expanded field.

GH: When you say it was 'unsuccessful', is this because it didn't work at the time or because now the terms have changed? Was it very personal?

AW: I don't think it would work now either. It was almost wilfully obscure; it wasn't even particularly personal, I think it was just not very accommodating.

GH: In more recent years, have you had any urge to make bigger work, perhaps for a specific site?

AW: The only one I've done relatively recently was at the Camden Arts Centre, in 1982. And I don't know if that worked either. It was made of a series of brass cones, strapped on trees, a little like loudspeakers or beacons.

GH: Obviously an invitation like the one for Dean Clough offers a unique opportunity to stretch your vocabulary, to make use of new materials and greater resources. Did you ever feel it was also something of an imposition, pushing you beyond your normal practice?

AW: I saw it as an opportunity to work quite outside the way that I normally operate. I think that happened - perhaps more than I would have liked. In some places I felt I did lose control at various points, the whole thing about having work fabricated is so different from making it yourself. I have a fantastic relationship with a couple of firms in London, who have made a few pieces for me: they just know, or maybe they don't, but at every point where there's a query or a problem I will go and see it and discuss it and sort it out. And there were times in the making of this work where I think that didn't happen, either because assumptions were made or because I simply wasn't there to see how things were being done.

GH: That sounds like a logistical problem. Isn't there also an inherent difficulty reproducing the quality of your work as a studio artist, achieving the same hand-crafted, touched quality which has been characteristic of it? At least until recent pieces like 'Displace' and 'Tidal', which have been fabricated; couldn't they be translated into ...

AW: No, because the scale's completely different. I had almost entirely made those pieces in advance in the studio, using other materials; I knew exactly the scale I wanted, how they were going to be put together.

GH: So even if the surface didn't have your touch, the precise configuration of elements did.

AW: Yes. It's not quite as straightforward as that, though, because with all the pieces that have been made there's been a real element of surprise. There certainly was with 'Displace', when its two elements finally came together, because they had been made in two different factories. I hadn't predicted - and I didn't actually want to predict - what it would be like. That was Factor X, if you like. But the thing about the works made in Dean Clough is that it was all Factor X. I felt it was really touch and go a lot of the time, I felt I didn't know what was being made. I tried to put myself inside the work, even though it wasn't there. I simply had to imagine what it would be like.

GH: Can you describe the process of planning and making you went through?

AW: Well, it's a list of blunders, really. I suppose the whole installation began with the staircase piece ('Pulse', pp.66 & 67). I had never found that balcony straightforward, coming through the outer door, then the inner door, and looking down from it into the first space like from the prow of a ship.
I had to learn how to deal with the whole space. The first show I visited, after being invited to work there, was John Newling's, and after that I saw every show. I wasn't interested in the historical or sociological traces of the building that other artists had found quite rich - it didn't have that kind of appeal for me. At that time it was a far less beautiful space, a very problematic space, which it isn't now.

GH: What has changed?

AW: The back space has been extended so it's twice the length it was, and it was originally all painted white. They've sandblasted the walls back to stone, and the pillars to cast iron. The two spaces now offer a real physical contrast but combine beautifully: the first one is light, the second one is dark. I responded immediately to that because of qualities I found in my own work, which Lynne Cooke describes in terms of its dualities. I felt those in the space itself; not immediately, but slowly, a whole way of approaching it began to make sense. I was interested in its light, not in any facts about it. Except that I do find important the fact that the first space is where they used to look at the carpets they made in the old mill: it's a place of examination, of scrutiny.

GH: You seem to have reacted quite strongly not only to the light but to the other material qualities of both spaces. In the first room, the white polypropylene construction seems appropriate both to the quality of lightness and to the plastic skylights; in the second, you've responded not only to the darkness but to the metal, the brick, the warmth of the room. Did that just happen, as a normal use of your vocabulary?

AW: I don't know whether it just happened, but it wasn't conscious. It could sound like I made the work almost like furnishing, which is not true. It's perhaps not surprising that it turned out like that since those are the materials I've always used.

GH: If you're not interested in the history of the place, what does the term 'site-specific' mean to you? Would you be inclined to look mainly for a site's more formal qualities?

AW: I was interested in making sense of it, or re-making sense of it, or re-inventing another sense for it. Underneath the space runs a beck, that Kounellis used and Magdalena Jetelová is going to use, which I was really drawn to the first time I went there, the idea of a spinal column that runs beneath the whole building. But I simply couldn't use a feature that is so specific.

GH: Is there also a sense, at a site like that which may originally be very wealthy in associations, of their having been somehow exhausted by other artists? Two artists can't do the same thing.

AW: I think that's how I felt, that it had been mined by everybody in a different way and actually there were pretty thin pickings left, were I to look at it that way, but I decided from the beginning that I didn't want to. I think the thing I did retain about the underground beck was that I wanted a feeling of a kind of continuity, a way of going from one space onto the next space that wasn't simply moving from one room to another room. For the work to lead you through, in quite a specific way.

GH: Some of the concerns of your studio work could be related to architectural concerns. Like the ideas of transparency and opacity, of intrusion and expulsion. At Halifax it's not just a case of the arena being bigger, it also has a different quality: the shape is pre-determined, it has a ready-made character as a building. Did you find that helpful or restricting?

AW: I don't know what you mean, 'predetermined'.

GH: It has a shape and a history, even if you weren't so concerned with its specific history. That still seems to have interested you, it seems to have allowed you to extend some of the ideas that occur in your studio work. It's not as if you had made this work and taken it into any large space.

AW: I suppose that 'Pulse' was the toughest to do. I set myself a very tight brief for making it, I don't know why, but I was completely obsessed with it not doing particular things. I didn't want anything to be altered, in order to make the piece work. In the end what they had to do - to accommodate the hydraulic lift, to get the piece on - was to saw part of the handrail off and remove the last section of the wooden platform. All this happened when I was involved with the opening of the show in Liverpool. That was one thing that I was actually quite upset by, although it was too late to express my anxieties about it. Had I been there, I would have maybe said 'yes, okay, we'll do this', but it meant that the vertical part of the piece was in a different place, so the whole proportion of the work within the room was altered.

There are other things about that piece that I really don't like, but I think I always knew that that would be the case. Doorways had to be cut into it, totally destroying the thing so you can walk through it. But I didn't want to change the rules in order to make the piece more this or that. I wanted to work with the problem that was there, I was absolutely obsessed with sticking to the thing that I wanted to do. Which simply was to make the entrance to the space also a way of walking through the piece; of giving it an interiorness that has absolutely nothing to do with the way you see it when you're in the space looking back. So you become almost the subject of the piece as you walk in.

GH: But you don't know that until you come through.

AW: No, you don't know that until you've absorbed the whole show. In a way, I was thinking that the person walking through is actually rather like the meteorite (p.68). Except that the meteorite stays in its place.
The first week after 'Pulse' was installed I knew it was working, with the play of light, exactly how I wanted it to work. The week after that we had really low cloud for six days and it didn't budge, the whole room was completely flat and torpid. I thought, 'Oh Christ, this is a nightmare, this doesn't work' and I fell into the trap of thinking that it was a piece of sculpture that should work in any context. But of course it isn't: I'm very clear about that now. In fact it was only when the meteorite was set into the roof that it began to work again. I think that the two objects are completely symbiotic.
And then I began to worry about whether anybody else would see that. To make it easier, I had all the windows that face the road as you come in varnished out, made diffuse. The painters brushed varnish on and stippled it with sponges. I think it's really beautiful, it almost changes the space more than anything else because the whole room becomes sealed, and the outside world is really quite removed from it. The only point in the space where you encounter the outside world in the way we normally do is through the pane of plexiglass that holds the meteorite. I think a lot of people still won't see it, but I think it's made as clear as it possibly could be.

GH: The potato/meteorite image of 'Infinities' (p.69) is a very striking one, having two such contrasting images given a single body. How did that come about?

AW: I'd made some very small pieces using tectites, which are the result of what happens when a meteorite hits land. But in using them I've never referred to their origins, where they come from, the kind of journey that they've been on in order to reach earth, which I find really fascinating. I find the whole galaxy difficult to comprehend. I saw that meteorite quite a long time ago in a particular shop in London. I almost bought it, but as a thing it just seemed too expensive to have. Working in Halifax I suddenly had this need to have a meteorite, so we phoned round everywhere in the North of England to find one that day; but of course you can't do that, they're incredibly rare. So I bought the one I'd seen before. A week later, by coincidence, I was driving home down the A1, and there was a story on the news about a man in Wolverhampton who'd heard this strange noise, and a one and a half pound meteorite had crashed into a bush in his garden and it was still warm when he picked it up. That was so exciting - it's apparently only the fifth one to fall in this country that's been recorded since the Second World War.

Suddenly everything began to clarify itself but I knew there was a problem in using something as arcane as a meteorite, which just looks at first like a twisted piece of metal. Actually it's very beautiful, it's like a man's head in some ways. Having decided on the place where it was going to be, it seemed a hell of a long way up, it could be a piece of chewing gum: I knew I also had to replicate it to make it more physically accessible. I used to sit in the studio all day figuring out what to do with this theoretical replica meteorite, cast in bronze or whatever. Then I was driving round near Hebden Bridge one afternoon listening to a radio programme, about children's science books. The first one mentioned was 'Where am I in Outer Space?', and the second one was 'What is my Body?'. Suddenly I realised that was the connection, to bring the meteorite right into one's self, to relate it to the interior of one's body. Then I thought of having it inside something that resembled an organ.... I don't know exactly how I came upon the idea of using the potato but that turned very quickly into the idea of having the meteorite inside a potato shape. The potato seemed incredibly resonant, being a cell, the way it reproduces itself, and the fact that it grows underground, in darkness, which in a sense is the same as the meteorite.

GH: It's just a bigger field.

AW: Exactly. The meteorite comes from darkness through to light. When the idea was suggested that it could be set in solid resin then I suddenly saw the way they could be, the way they are now. It's like a tadpole, like the birth of something but also the end of something, and it's also exposure and immersion all in one place. Placed simply in the spaces which used to be windows between the two rooms, they behave like lenses and reflect the whole room, upside down. I think they're the fulcrum, in the way one space leads into the other one.

GH: I'd like to ask you about the work called 'Stain' (p.71) in that second room: were there specific problems - or things that attracted you - about the requirement to work on such a large scale with a relatively familiar form? Your sculptures 'Into the Brass' and 'Bearing' are in many ways similar to 'Stain': how big a difference is there between working with five square metres of cloth and fifty?

AW: Logistically it's much more complicated. We almost didn't get that cloth because the mill went into receivership just before it was delivered, but then deals were done in car parks.

GH: You told me before that you couldn't see it, that it was difficult to test out.

AW: If ever I made another piece as large as that with cloth - and I can say now that I wouldn't, but who knows? - I would take more liberties. Probably in every case I would behave quite differently about working with material on a larger scale.

GH: How?

AW: I should have insisted in the mill that I lay all of the cloth out on the floor to see what it looked like. My first thought when it arrived was that it was too thin, that it wasn't dense enough on the floor. That piece ended up relatively unchanged from the kind of ideas I had about it from the start, but it was an age before all the

elements were together and when they were, I realised that I'd had no idea what it would be like. Or how the cloth would behave, or what I even wanted it to do. So when it was put together I thought it was absolutely terrible, a complete shambles, and thought the whole thing was going to have to come off again.

GH: Did you change your mind?

AW: I spent days kicking it around, and I think I just made sense of it: because I hadn't thought about it having any sense in a physical way, like what would happen to the cloth when it came down the side, or before it came out... it just didn't have any meaning at all.

GH: You made other changes on site: I thought the elements of 'Assembly' (p.72) were meant to be much closer together.

AW: I wasn't surprised at that change. That piece was always quite elastic in the way that it was put together. One part could have been inside the other or they could have been separated further. In some ways that was the most exciting piece to do, because I felt I had more control over it, it was smaller and much more familiar. The PVC piece was made by someone who had made other pieces for me, so I was absolutely confident how it was going to be, and had seen it set up.

GH: Do you finally see what you've done at Dean Clough, if it has to be described or limited, as large-scale sculpture, or as installation, or as architecture?

AW: Well I think certainly the first room is an installation; I wouldn't want that to go anywhere else. I think as you move through the spaces your relationship with the work changes a lot. Until, at the end, you're dealing with something that's quite different from the piece that you were dealing with at first, it's a much more conventional relationship. In a way that's very satisfying, this definite progression through the space to the last piece which itself goes in and out and perhaps sends you back the other way.

GH: You've had a unique chance to see newly commissioned work next to a mini-retrospective, at the Tate Gallery in Liverpool. Have you made comparisons, does one enhance the other for you?

AW: The work at Dean Clough demands a completely different time span. I think it's a very different kind of experience, going into each of those spaces. The show at Liverpool is much more conventional, things are given a recognisable space and context. It's like you follow the dotted line.

GH: At the Tate, your name is on the door, the literature is helpful, people know what they're getting into. At Halifax it's the opposite: you walk in and are immediately upon the space, with little to prepare you.

AW: I know some people call that elitist, but I like it because I think the whole space encourages people to stay a long time. It's partly to do with the location, since many people travel quite a long way to go there and so probably want to spend a long time, and maybe want to go out and come back and really make sense of it. I think the place is geared to the art, not to a kind of consumerism. That's the great thing about it, that and the opportunity it gives to an artist to do something that otherwise they wouldn't - in my case couldn't do in my studio.

GH: Do you think there's a danger that it might encourage a kind of theatricality, both in the character of the building and also the demands on you, knowing that people are coming a long way and expect to have their breath taken away?

AW: Yes, I've wondered how spectacular it need be and think my worries about the light and the weather are probably located in that. Without the sun it's actually very low-key: although the piece is still there it isn't brought to life in the same way. And I think it is spectacular: slowly spectacular. I wanted it to be a very different kind of experience from Liverpool. Almost like a journey that you embark on between those two rooms, and not simply looking at pieces of work that might or might not be related.

GH: You set the tone by involving the spectator right from the start.

AW: Yes, I think that show – and also probably the show in Liverpool – is about 'immersion' as well as about 'exposure'. I don't think you can have one without the other.

GH: Do you feel there's anything the experience at Dean Clough has substantially added to the meaning of your work? The kind of thing that I would suggest is that most of your earlier sculpture has been very tightly to do with itself, they're definite pieces, you walk around them, they've got a kind of force-field. As you've said, the first work at Dean Clough, 'Pulse', is entirely different; do you think any of its qualities will be developed in the future?

AW: I don't know. I do feel that the work has really expanded. The pieces work together, not simply as a series of reflections or relationships that are there as evidence of particular preoccupations or obsessions but because they're actually built into each piece. The experience of all of them is richer than the experience of five separate pieces.
I really don't know how it will change what I will do next. I couldn't say – I hope it does. I think it's wonderful to be shaken up, for whatever reason, and I think it's done that. I've shaken up what I've done a lot in the last year, but I think this has done as much as anything.

1   *Pulse* 1991
    Polypropylene
    5850 x 5430 x 2145mm

2   Iron meteorite
    Found Henbury, Australia, 1931
    weight 75gm
    set in plexiglass
    1550 x 495mm

3   *Infinities* 1991
    Meteorite cast in bronze set in resin
    cast from potato
    Edition of five
    107 x 65 x 45mm

4   *Stain* 1991
    Steel, rubber and woollen cloth
    2970 x 10,000 x 4850mm

5   *Assembly* 1991
    Steel and PVC
    1230 X 1740 X 5470mm

Interior view, *Pulse*

Pulse 1991

Iron Meteorite

Infinities 1991

Installation view of *Assembly* and *Stain*

Stain 1991

Assembly 1991

ALISON WILDING

Born: 1948, Blackburn, Lancashire
Lives and works in London

EDUCATION

1967-70   Ravensbourne College of Art and Design, Bromley, Kent
1970-73   Royal College of Art, London

ONE PERSON EXHIBITIONS

1970   Young Friends of the Tate Gallery, Pear Place, London
1976   AIR Gallery, London
1982   Kettle's Yard Gallery, Cambridge
1983   Salvatore Ala Gallery, New York
1985   Salvatore Ala Gallery, Milan
          Serpentine Gallery, London
1986   Salvatore Ala Gallery, New York
1987   Galleri Lang, Malmo
          Karsten Schubert Ltd, London
1987-88   Projects: Museum of Modern Art, New York
1988   Gallerie Wanda Reiff, Maastricht
          Asher/Faure, Los Angeles
1988-89   Karsten Schubert Ltd, London
1989   Hirschl & Adler Modern, New York
1989   Mala Galerija, Moderna Galerija, Ljubljana
1990   Karsten Schubert Ltd, London

GROUP SHOWS

1973   Clare Court, Trinity College, Cambridge
1975   SPACE Open Studios, London
1977   Riverside Studios, London
1979   *New Sculpture★:* Ikon Gallery, Birmingham
          55 Wapping Artists: London
1980   *Eight Women Artists★:* Acme Gallery, London
          Whitechapel Open: Whitechapel Art Gallery, London
          Wapping Artists Open Studios: London
1981   *G.L.A.A. Awards 1981:* Woodland Art Gallery, London
          Wapping Artists 1981: London
1982   *Whitechapel Open:* Whitechapel Art Gallery, London
          Le Sculpture/La Sculpture: Eton College, Windsor
          Wapping Artists Open Studio Exhibition: London
          Collezione Inglese★: Scuola di San Pasquale, Venice
          Sculpture in the Garden★: Camden Arts Centre, London
          Paris Biennale★
          St Paul's Gallery, Leeds
1983   *Figures and Objects★:* John Hansard Gallery, University of
          Southampton, Southampton
          Whitechapel Open: Whitechapel Art Gallery, London
          Tolly Cobbold/Eastern Arts 4th National Exhibition
          (prizewinner): Fitzwilliam Museum, Cambridge, & tour
          The Sculpture Show★: Arts Council of Great Britain,
          Serpentine and Hayward Galleries, London
          Transformations: New Sculpture from Britain★: XVII
          Biennale de São Paulo: Museu de Arte Moderna, Rio de
          Janiero; Museo de Arte Moderno, Mexico; Museu Calouste
          Gulbenkian, Lisbon

★The asterisk marking certain titles in this list of group shows indicates that a catalogue was published to accompany the exhibition.

1984   *Collezione Inglese:* Scuola di San Pasquale, Venice
          The British Art Show★ : Arts Council of Great Britain,
          touring Birmingham, Edinburgh, Sheffield and
          Southampton

1985   *The British Show★:* Art Gallery of Western Australia;
          Art Gallery of New South Wales; Queensland Art Gallery;
          National Gallery, Wellington
          10 Years at AIR: AIR Gallery, London
          Nuove Trame dell'Arte★: Castello Colona, Genazanno
          Anniottanta★: Galleria Comunale d'Arte Moderna, Bologna
          (Chiostri della Loggetta, Lombardesca, Ravenna section)
          Synonyms for Sculpture★ : Neue Galerie am
          Landesmuseum Joannuem, Graz
          The Irish Exhibition of Living Art: Guinness Hop Store,
          Dublin

1986   Burnett Miller Gallery, Los Angeles
          Between Object and Image: Ministerio de Cultera and the
          British Council, Palacio de Velasquez, Madrid;
          Fundació Caixa de Pensions, Barcelona;
          Museo de Bellas Artes, Bilbao
          Sculpture: Nine Artists from Britain★: Louisiana Museum of
          Modern Art, Humlebaek
          Art and Alchemy: Venice Biennale XLII★: Venice
          Prospect '86★: Frankfurter Kunstverein
          Jeffrey Dennis, Alan Green, Alison Wilding: Third Eye
          Centre, Glasgow
          Third Generation Women: Canterbury Fringe Festival,
          Canterbury
          Domenico Bianchi, Antony Gormley, Roberto Pace,
          Alison Wilding: Galleria Salvatore Ala, Milan

1987   *Casting an Eye:* Co-selected with Richard Deacon:
          Cornerhouse, Manchester
          Current Affairs: British Painting and Sculpture in the 1980s:
          Museum of Modern Art, Oxford, & toured by the British
          Council to Mücsarnok, Budapest; Národni Galerie,
          Prague; Zecheta, Warsaw
          Art Brittiskt 1980 - Tal: Liljevalchs Konsthall,
          Stockholm; Sara Hildén Museum, Tampere
          Beelden en Banieren: Fort Asperen, Acquoy
          Atlantic Sculpture: Art Centre, College of Design, Pasadena
          Viewpoint – British Art of the 80s: Museum of Modern Art,
          Musées Royaux de Beaux Arts de Belgique, Brussels
          Edinburgh International Festival: Reason and Emotion in
          Contemporary Art: Royal Scottish Academy, Edinburgh
          Lead: Hirschl and Adler Modern, New York

1988   *British Art - The Literate Link★:* Asher/Faure, Los Angeles
        All That Matters: Alison Wilding, Tom Dean, Remo Salvatori,
        Richard Deacon★: Art Gallery of Windsor, Ontario; Mendel
        Art Gallery, Saskatoon; Saidye Bronfman Centre, Montreal
        Roche Court Sculpture Garden, Salisbury
        Starlit Waters: British Sculpture. An International Art★: Tate
        Gallery, Liverpool
        Brittanica: 30 Ans de Sculpture★: Musée des Beaux Arts
        André Malraux, Le Havre; L'Ecole D'Architecture de
        Normandie, Darnétal; Musée D'Evreux, Ancien Évêché,
        Evreux; Museum Van Hedendaagse Kunst, Antwerp
        Vanitas★: Norwich School of Art Gallery, Norwich
        British Now - Sculpture et Autres Dessins★: Musée d'art
        contemporain, Montreal
        Cinquième Ateliers Internationaux des Pays de la Loire★:
        Abbaye Royale de Fontevraud
1989   *Istanbul, 2nd Biennale:* Istanbul
1990   *Now For The Future: Purchases for the Arts Council Collection*
        since 1984★: Hayward Gallery, London
        Rebecca Horn, Willi Kopf, Richard Long, Alison Wilding:
        Centre d'art contemporain du Domaine de Kerguehennec
1991   *Pulsio:* Fundació Caixa de Pensions, Barcelona

        CATALOGUES
        published for one person exhibitions

1985   Lynne Cooke
        Alison Wilding
        Serpentine Gallery, London

1987   Gray Watson
        Alison Wilding: Sculptures
        Karsten Schubert Ltd, London

1988   Marjorie Allthorpe-Guyton
        Alison Wilding: Sculptures 1987/88
        Karsten Schubert Ltd, London

1989   Marjorie Allthorpe-Guyton
        Alison Wilding
        Hirschl and Adler Modern, New York